Lots of Legs

Written by Claire Llewellyn

Illustrated by Clive Goodyer

Animals with lots of legs

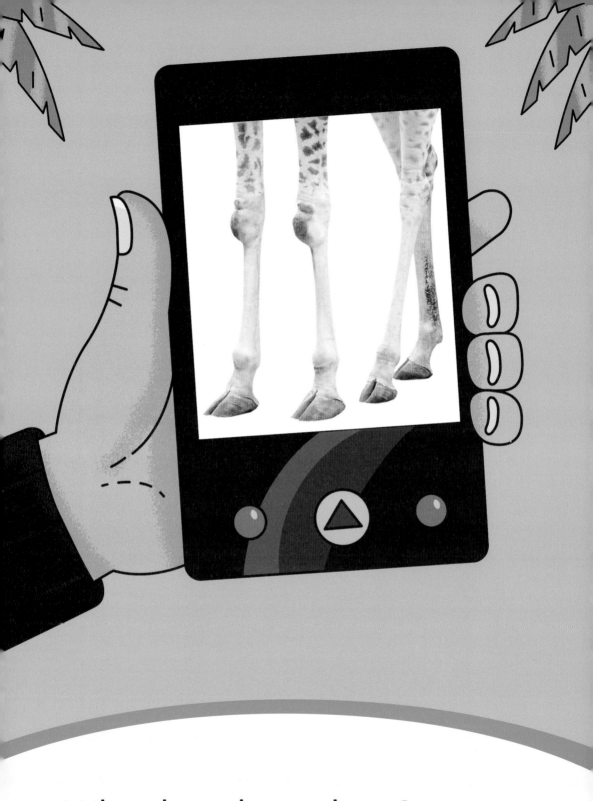

Who has long legs?

I do!
I have a long neck as well.

Who has big, thick legs?

I do!
I have big teeth as well.

Who has legs with lots
of dots?

I do!
I have dots on my back
as well.

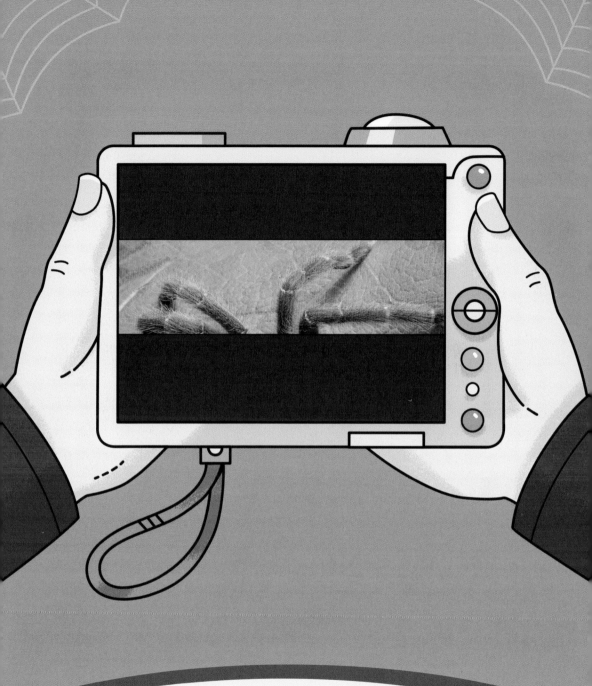

Who has legs with
lots of fuzz?

I do!
I have **lots** of legs!

Who has legs like this?

We do!

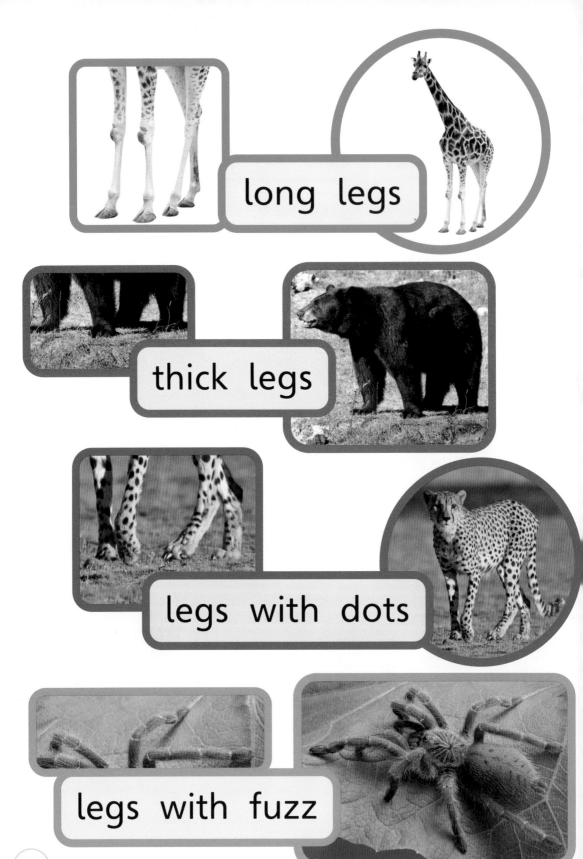

long legs

thick legs

legs with dots

legs with fuzz